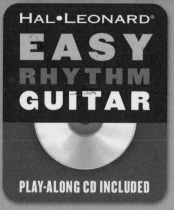

HAL•LEONARD
EASY RHYTHM GUITAR
PLAY-ALONG CD INCLUDED

CHRISTMAS SONGS

W9-BNP-071

ISBN 978-1-4234-5654-4

HAL•LEONARD®
CORPORATION

7777 W. BLUEMOUND RD. P.O. BOX 13819 MILWAUKEE, WI 53213

Visit Hal Leonard Online at
www.halleonard.com

Blue Christmas

Words and Music by Billy Hayes and Jay Johnson

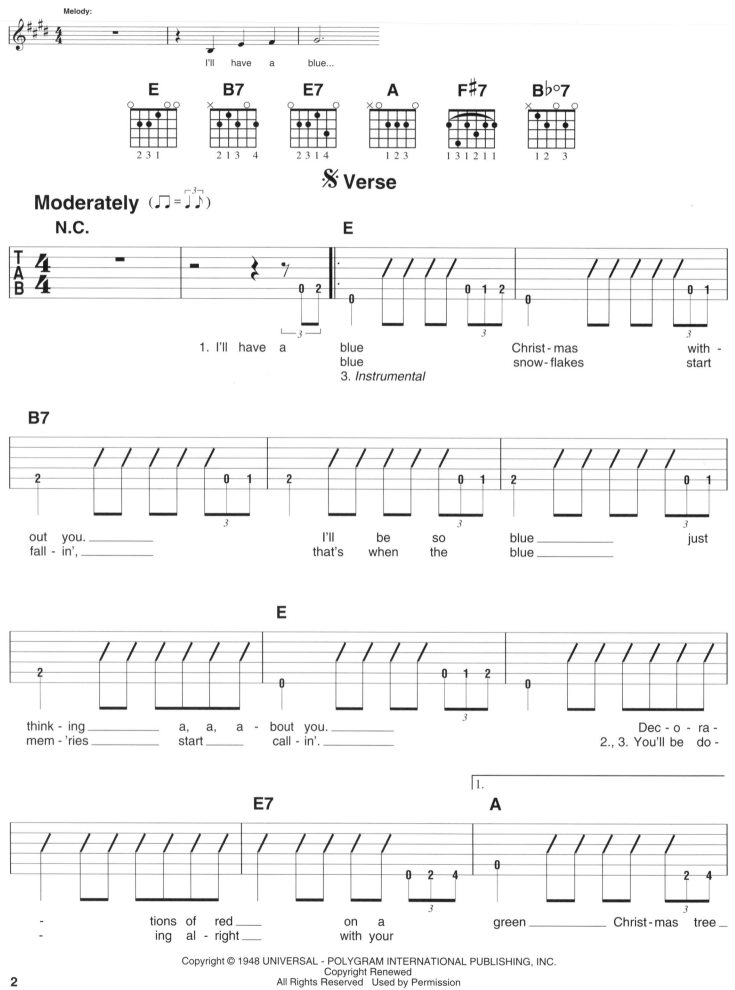

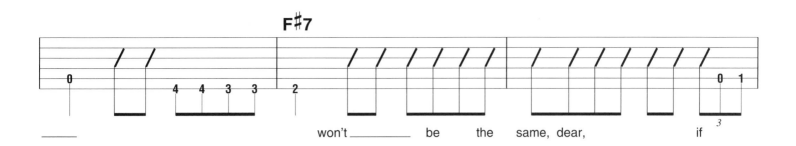

won't ___ be the same, dear, if

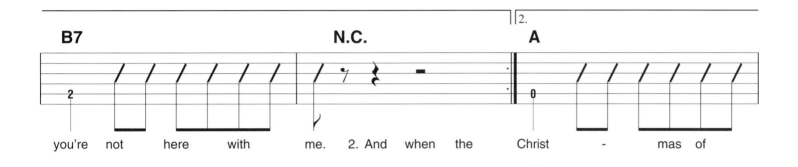

you're not here with me. 2. And when the Christ - mas of

To Coda ⊕

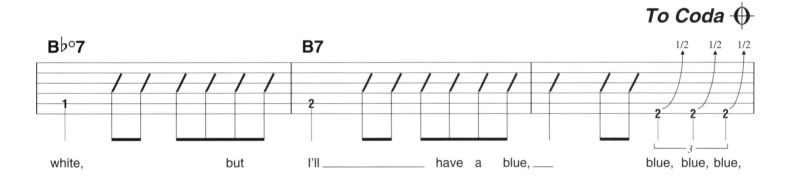

white, but I'll ___ have a blue, ___ blue, blue, blue,

D.S. al Coda
(take 2nd ending)

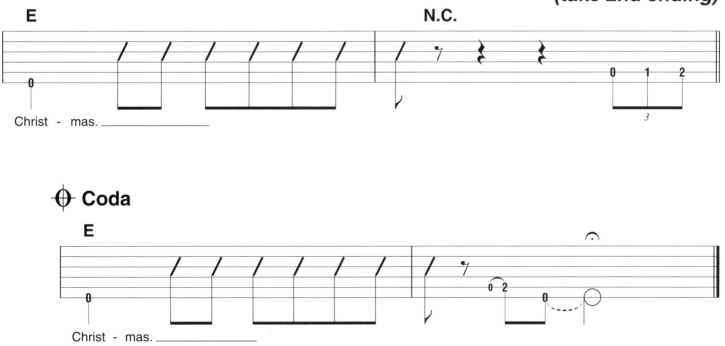

Christ - mas. ___

⊕ Coda

E

Christ - mas. ___

Do You Hear What I Hear

TRACK 3

Words and Music by Noel Regney and Gloria Shayne

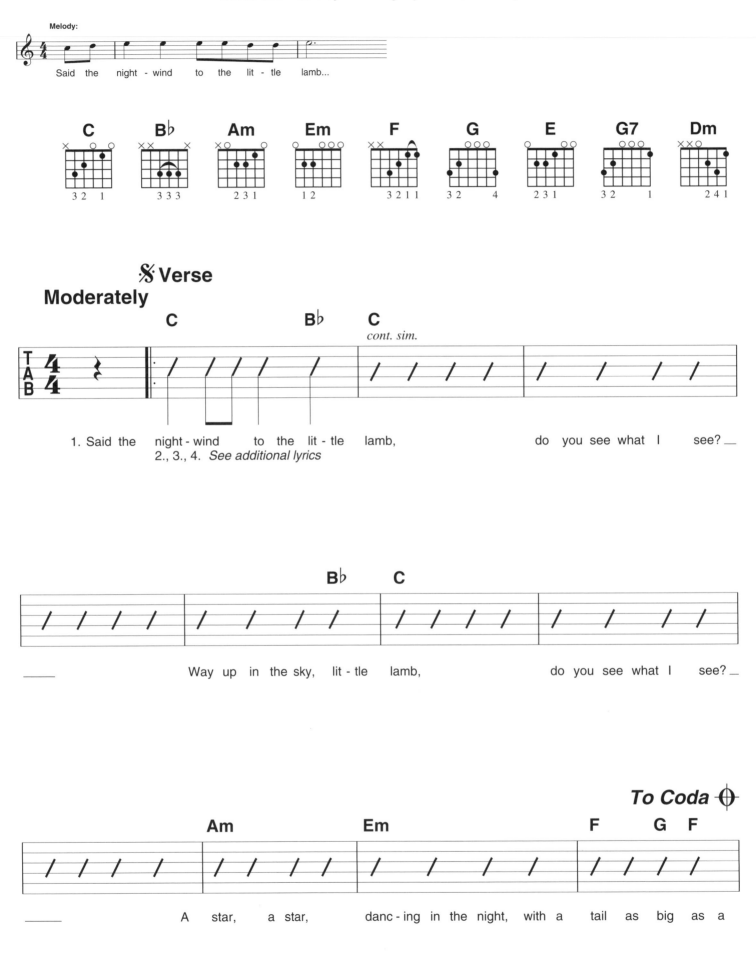

1. Said the night-wind to the lit-tle lamb,
2., 3., 4. *See additional lyrics*

do you see what I see?___

Way up in the sky, lit-tle lamb, do you see what I see?___

A star, a star, danc-ing in the night, with a tail as big as a

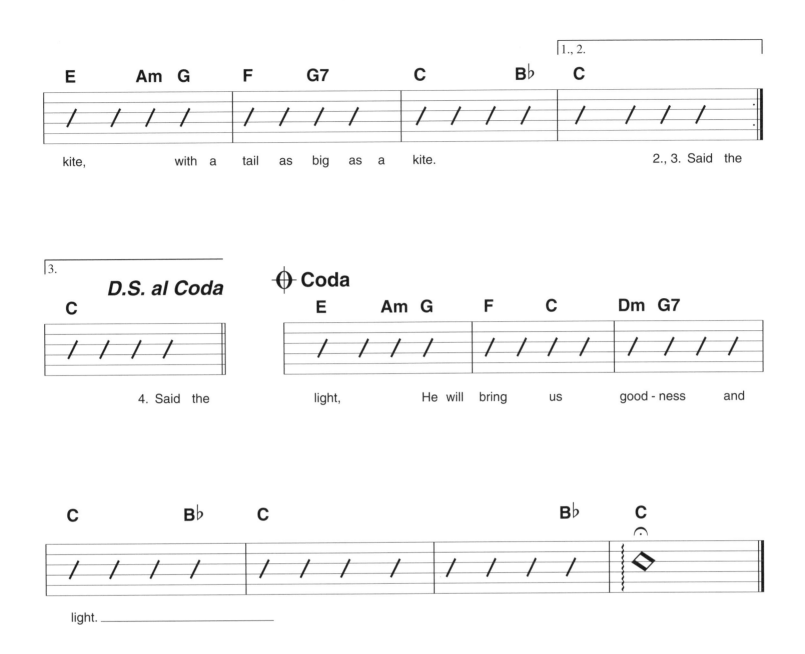

Additional Lyrics

2. Said the little lamb to the shepherd boy,
   Do you hear what I hear?
   Ringing through the sky, shepherd boy,
   Do you hear what I hear?
   A song, a song, high above the tree,
   With a voice as big as the sea,
   With a voice as big as the sea.

3. Said the shepherd boy to the mighty king,
   Do you know what I know?
   In your palace warm, mighty king,
   Do you know what I know?
   A Child, a Child shivers in the cold,
   Let us bring Him silver and gold,
   Let us bring Him silver and gold.

4. Said the king to the people ev'rywhere,
   Listen to what I say!
   Pray for peace, people ev'rywhere,
   Listen to what I say!
   The Child, the Child, sleeping in the night;
   He will bring us goodness and light,
   He will bring us goodness and light.

Frosty the Snowman

Words and Music by Steve Nelson and Jack Rollins

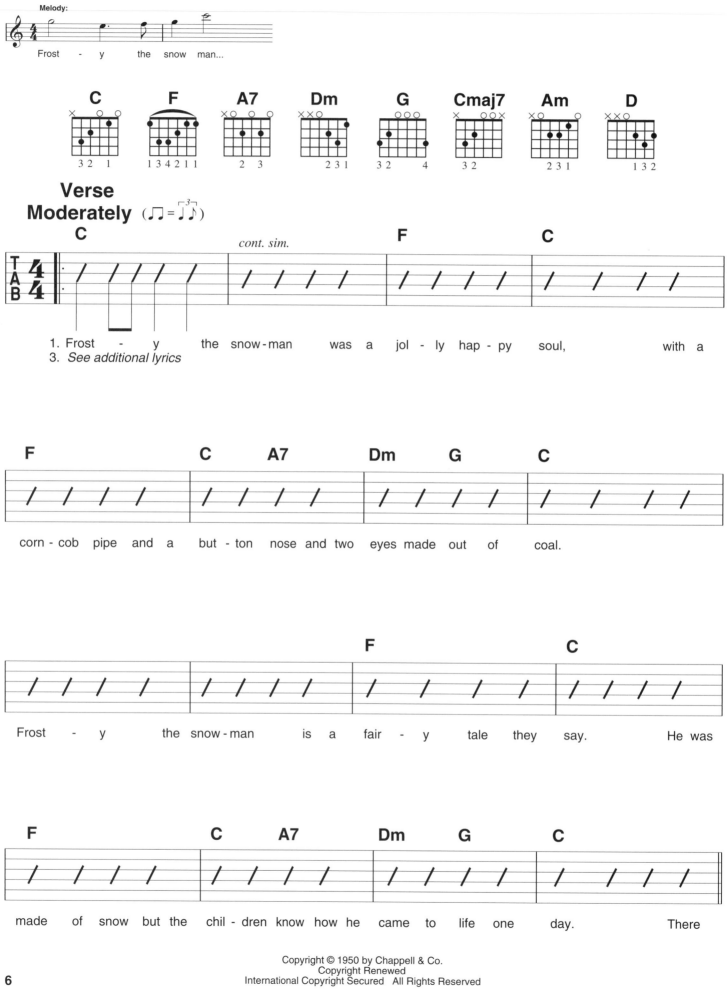

Melody:

Frost - y   the   snow   man...

C   F   A7   Dm   G   Cmaj7   Am   D

Verse
Moderately

C   cont. sim.   **F**   **C**

1. Frost - y   the   snow-man   was   a   jol - ly   hap - py   soul,   with a
3. *See additional lyrics*

F   **C**   **A7**   **Dm**   **G**   **C**

corn - cob   pipe   and a   but - ton   nose and two   eyes made   out   of   coal.

                              F   **C**

Frost - y   the   snow - man   is   a   fair - y   tale   they   say.   He was

F   **C**   **A7**   **Dm**   **G**   **C**

made   of   snow   but the   chil - dren   know   how   he   came   to   life   one   day.   There

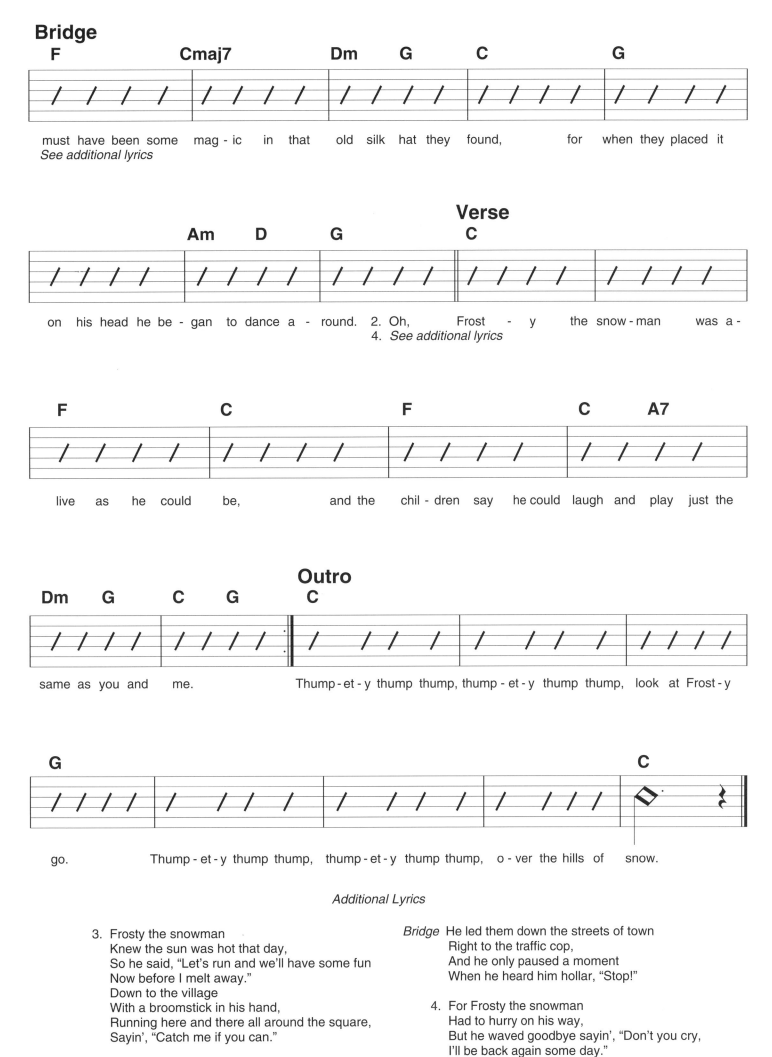

Bridge

F   Cmaj7   Dm   G   C   G

must have been some   mag - ic   in   that   old   silk   hat they   found,   for   when they placed it
See additional lyrics

         Am   D   G   **Verse**
                           C

on   his   head he be - gan   to   dance a - round. 2. Oh,   Frost - y   the   snow - man   was a -
                                        4. *See additional lyrics*

F   C   F   C   A7

live   as   he   could   be,   and the   chil - dren   say   he could   laugh   and   play   just the

Dm   G   C   G   **Outro**
                          C

same   as   you   and   me.   Thump - et - y thump thump, thump - et - y thump thump,   look   at Frost - y

G   C

go.   Thump - et - y thump thump,   thump - et - y thump thump,   o - ver the hills of   snow.

Additional Lyrics

3. Frosty the snowman
    Knew the sun was hot that day,
    So he said, "Let's run and we'll have some fun
    Now before I melt away."
    Down to the village
    With a broomstick in his hand,
    Running here and there all around the square,
    Sayin', "Catch me if you can."

Bridge He led them down the streets of town
        Right to the traffic cop,
        And he only paused a moment
        When he heard him holler, "Stop!"

4. For Frosty the snowman
    Had to hurry on his way,
    But he waved goodbye sayin', "Don't you cry,
    I'll be back again some day."

Happy Xmas
(War Is Over)

Words and Music by John Lennon and Yoko Ono

Melody:
So this is Christ mas...

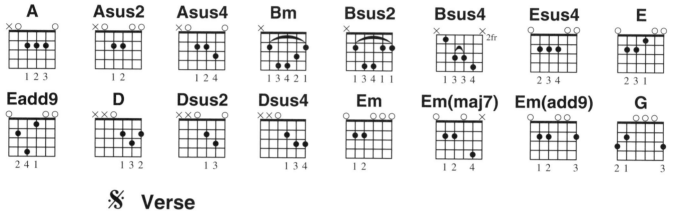

Moderately

𝄋 Verse

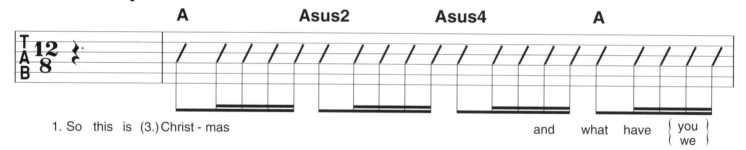

1. So this is (3.)Christ - mas   and   what   have { you }
                                                                               { we }

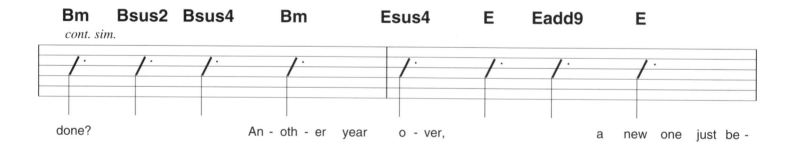

cont. sim.

done?   An - oth - er year   o - ver,   a   new   one   just   be -

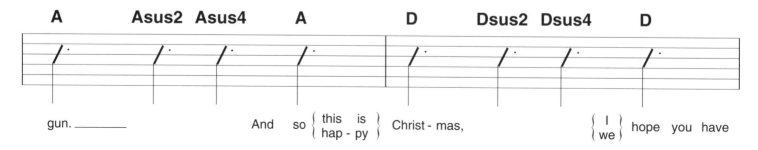

gun. _____   And   so { this is } Christ - mas,   { I } hope you have
                              { hap - py }   { we }

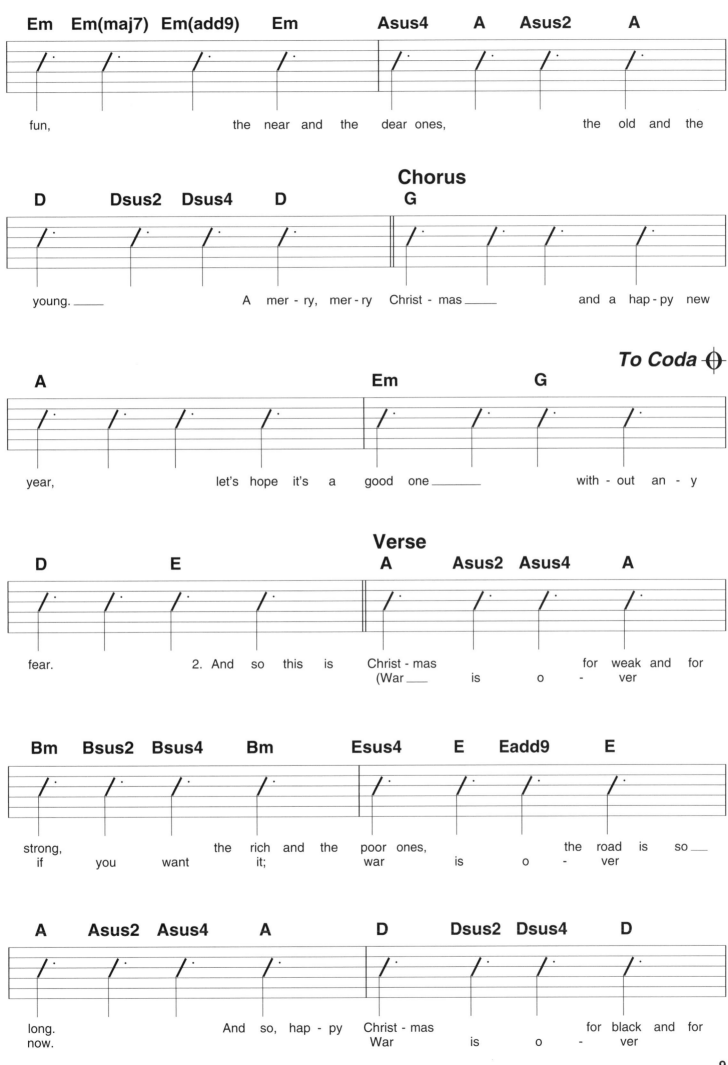

Em Em(maj7) Em(add9)   Em   Asus4   A   Asus2   A

fun,   the near and the   dear ones,   the old and the

D   Dsus2   Dsus4   D   **Chorus**
                                          G

young. ____   A mer - ry, mer - ry Christ - mas ____   and a hap - py new

To Coda ⊕

A   Em   G

year,   let's hope it's a   good one ____   with - out an - y

Verse

D   E   A   Asus2 Asus4   A

fear.   2. And so this is Christ - mas   for weak and for
                                     (War ___   is   o -   ver

Bm   Bsus2   Bsus4   Bm   Esus4   E   Eadd9   E

strong,   the rich and the poor ones,   the road is so ___
if   you   want   it;   war   is   o   -   ver

A   Asus2   Asus4   A   D   Dsus2   Dsus4   D

long.   And so, hap - py Christ - mas   for black and for
now.   War   is   o   -   ver

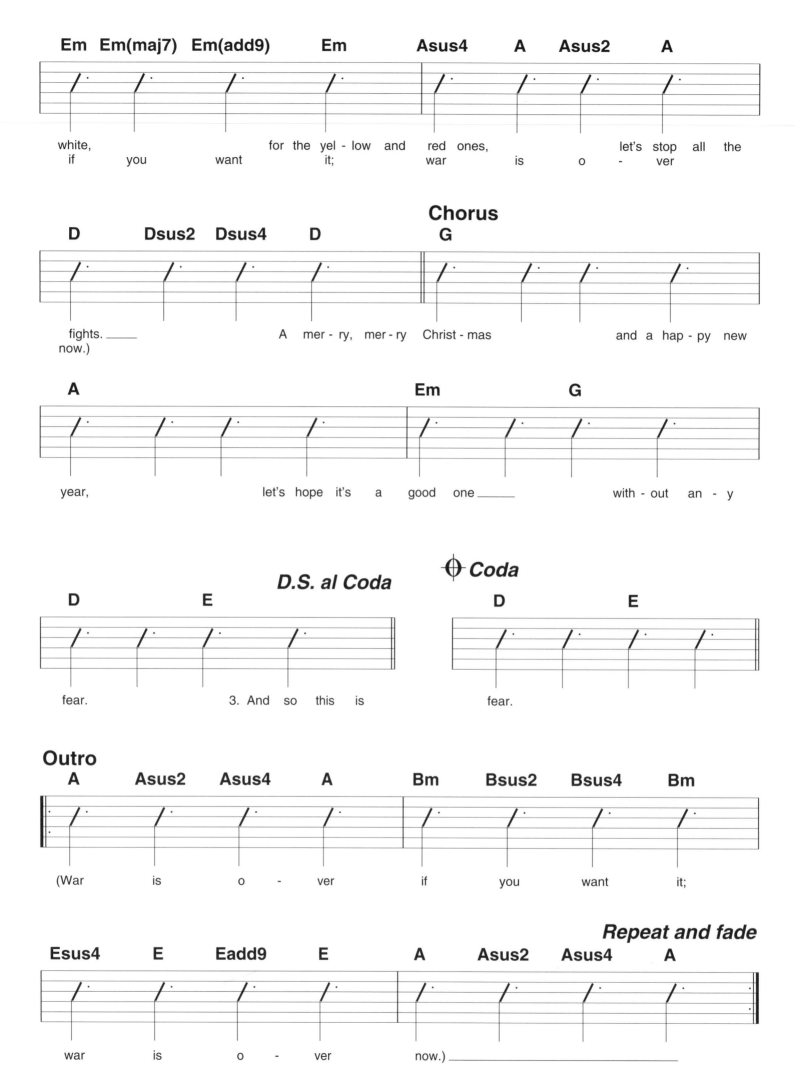

Jingle-Bell Rock

Words and Music by Joe Beal and Jim Boothe

Melody:

Jin gle bell, jin gle-bell, jin gle bell rock...

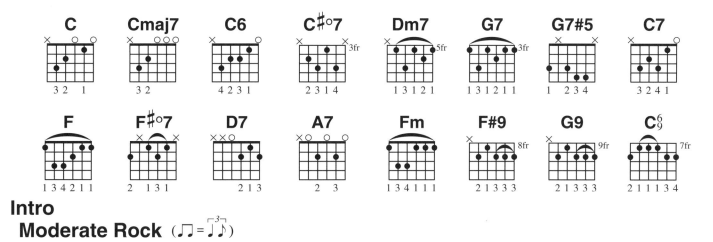

Intro
Moderate Rock

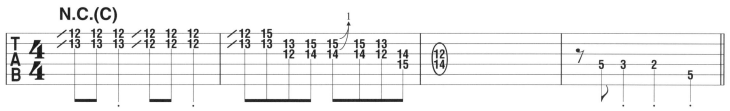

Verse

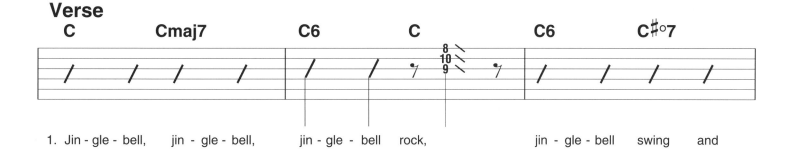

1. Jin-gle-bell, jin-gle-bell, jin-gle-bell rock, jin-gle-bell swing and

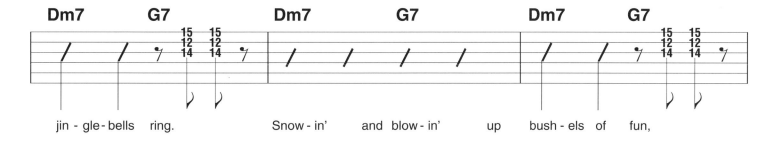

jin-gle-bells ring. Snow-in' and blow-in' up bush-els of fun,

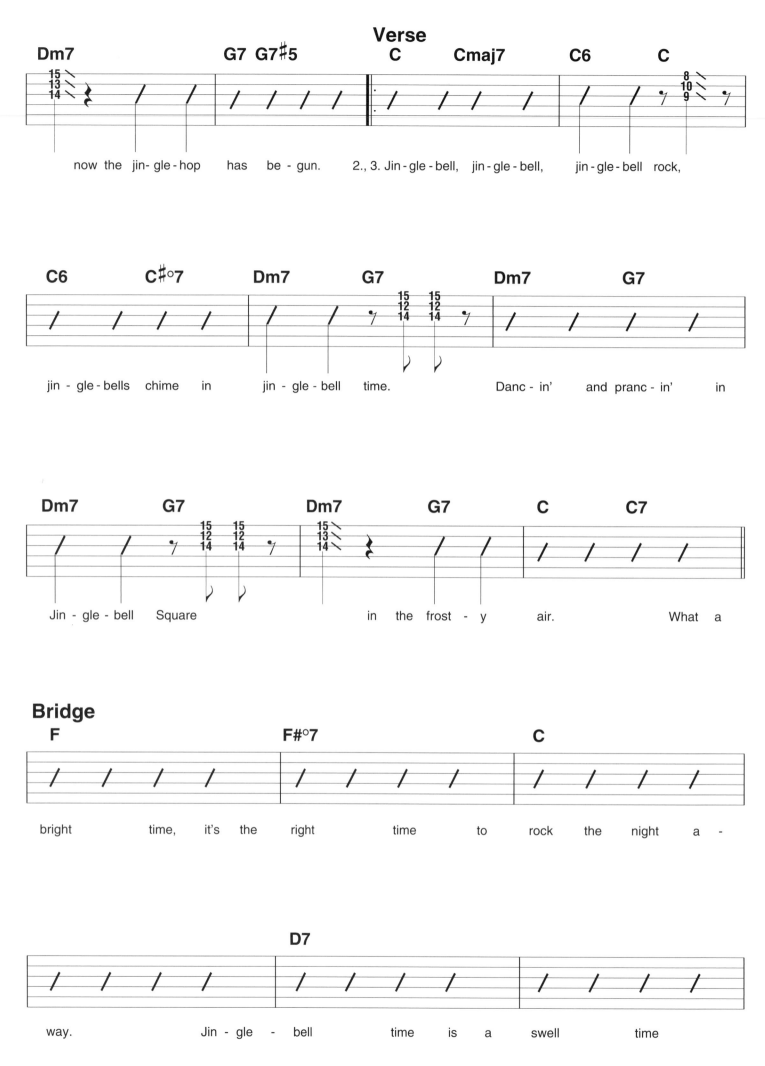

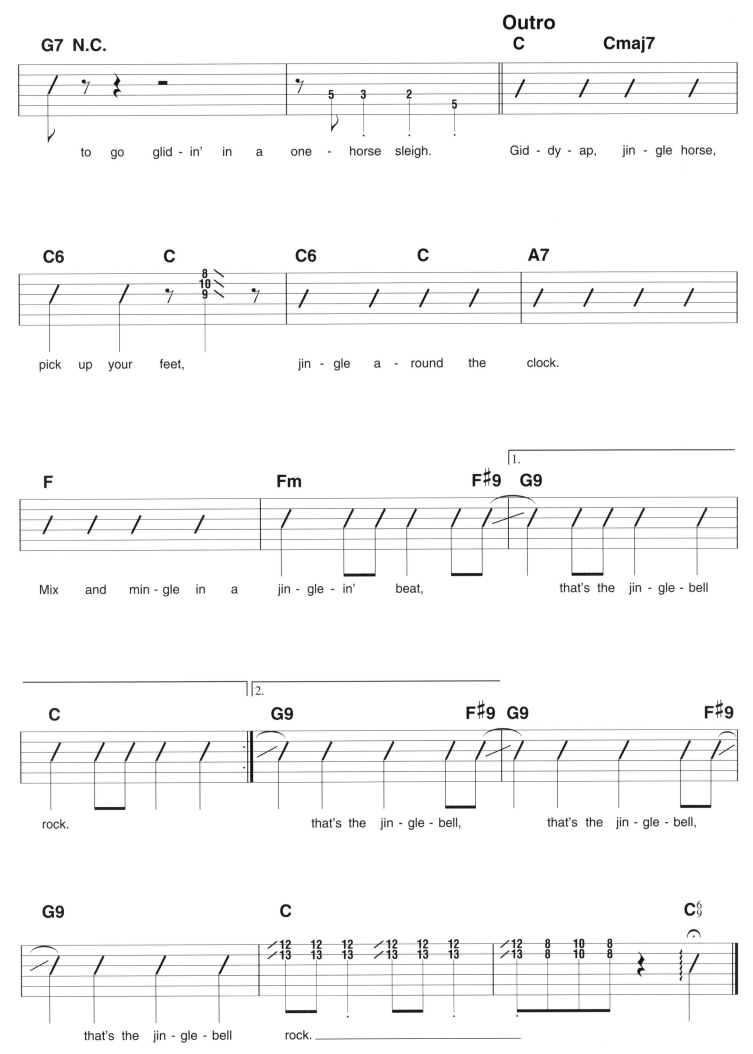

Outro

to go glid - in' in a one - horse sleigh. Gid - dy - ap, jin - gle horse,

pick up your feet, jin - gle a - round the clock.

Mix and min - gle in a jin - gle - in' beat, that's the jin - gle - bell

rock. that's the jin - gle - bell, that's the jin - gle - bell,

that's the jin - gle - bell rock.

Here Comes Santa Claus
(Right Down Santa Claus Lane)

Words and Music by Gene Autry and Oakley Haldeman

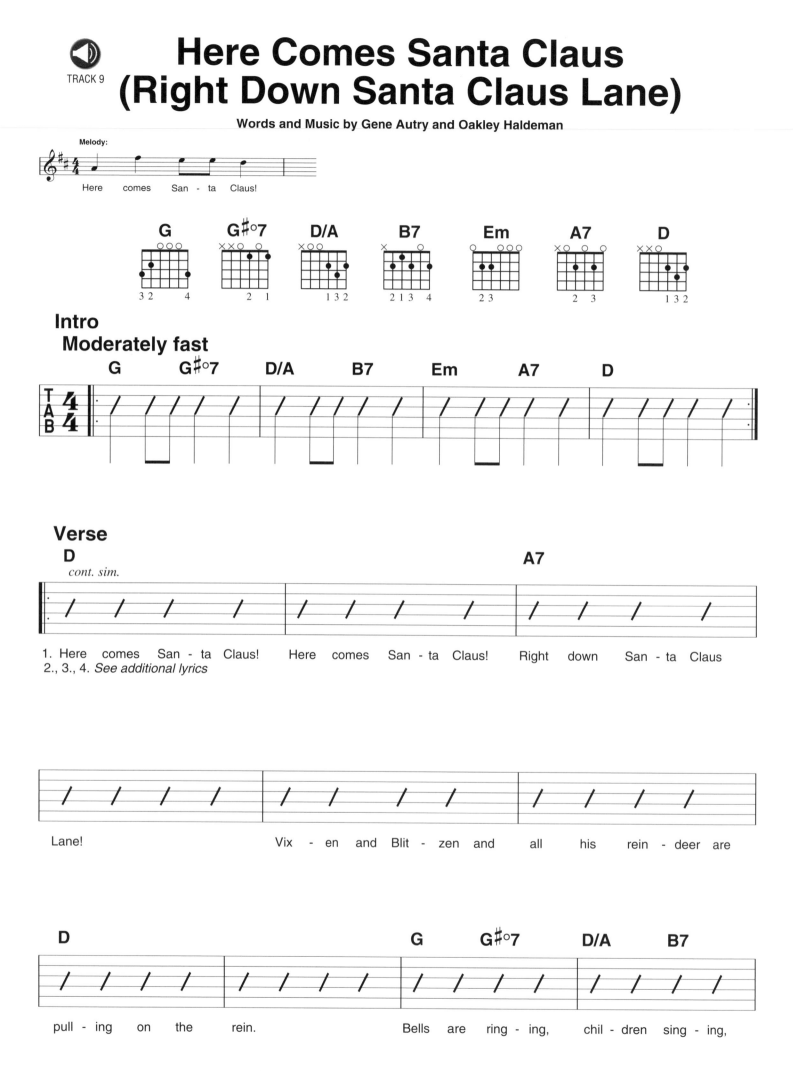

Intro
Moderately fast

Verse

1. Here comes San - ta Claus! Here comes San - ta Claus! Right down San - ta Claus
2., 3., 4. *See additional lyrics*

Lane!   Vix - en and Blit - zen and   all   his   rein - deer are

pull - ing on the rein.   Bells are ring - ing, chil - dren sing - ing,

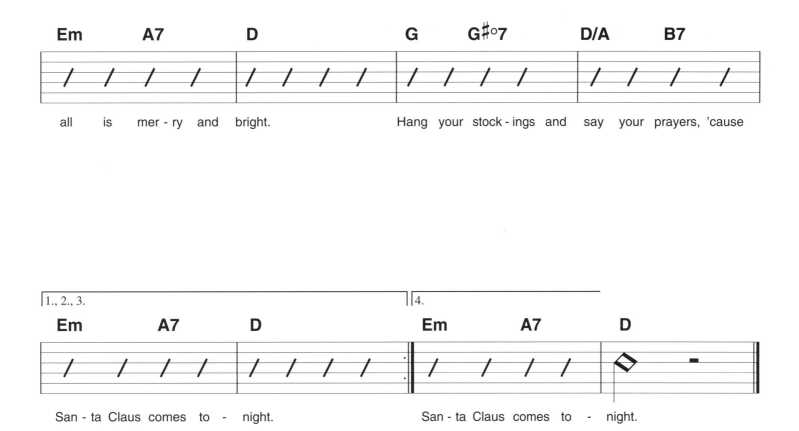

Em	A7	D	G	G#°7	D/A	B7

all   is   mer - ry   and   bright.   Hang   your   stock - ings   and   say   your   prayers, 'cause

1., 2., 3.

Em	A7	D

4.

Em	A7	D

San - ta Claus comes to - night.   San - ta Claus comes to - night.

Additional Lyrics

2. Here comes Santa Claus! Here comes Santa Claus!
Right down Santa Claus Lane!
He's got a bag that is filled with toys
For the boys and girls again.
Hear those sleigh bells jingle, jangle,
What a beautiful sight.
Jump in bed, cover up your head,
Santa Claus comes tonight.

3. Here comes Santa Claus! Here comes Santa Claus!
Right down Santa Claus Lane!
He doesn't care if you're rich or poor,
For he loves you just the same.
Santa knows that we're God's children;
That makes ev'rything right.
Fill your hearts with a Christmas cheer,
'Cause Santa Claus comes tonight.

4. Here comes Santa Claus! Here comes Santa Claus!
Right down Santa Claus Lane!
He'll come around when the chimes ring out;
Then it's Christmas morn again.
Peace on earth will come to all
If we just follow the light.
Let's give thanks to the Lord above,
Santa Claus comes tonight.

I Saw Mommy Kissing Santa Claus

Words and Music by Tommie Connor

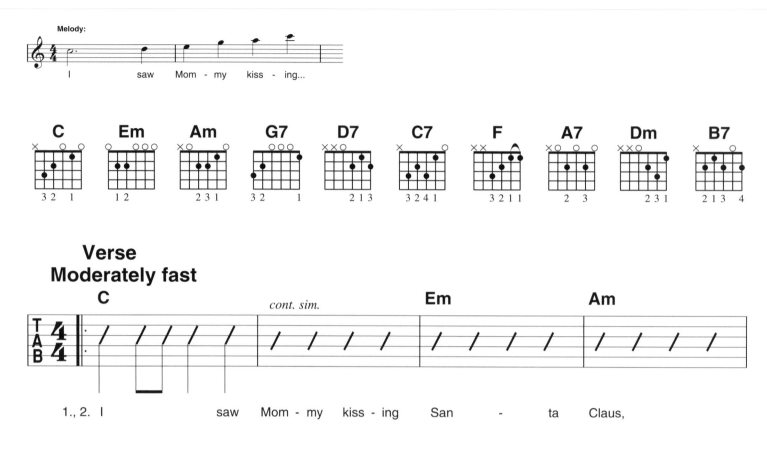

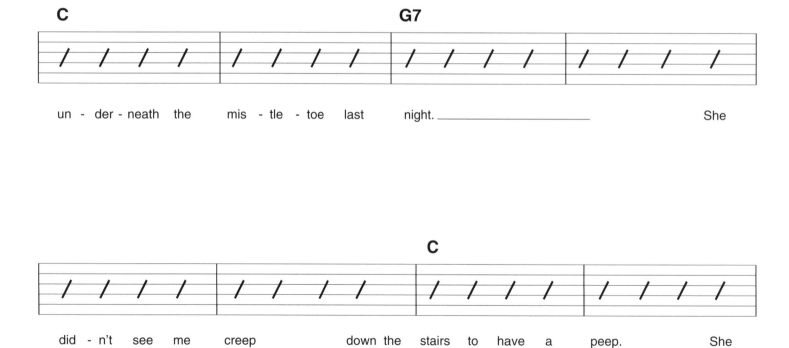

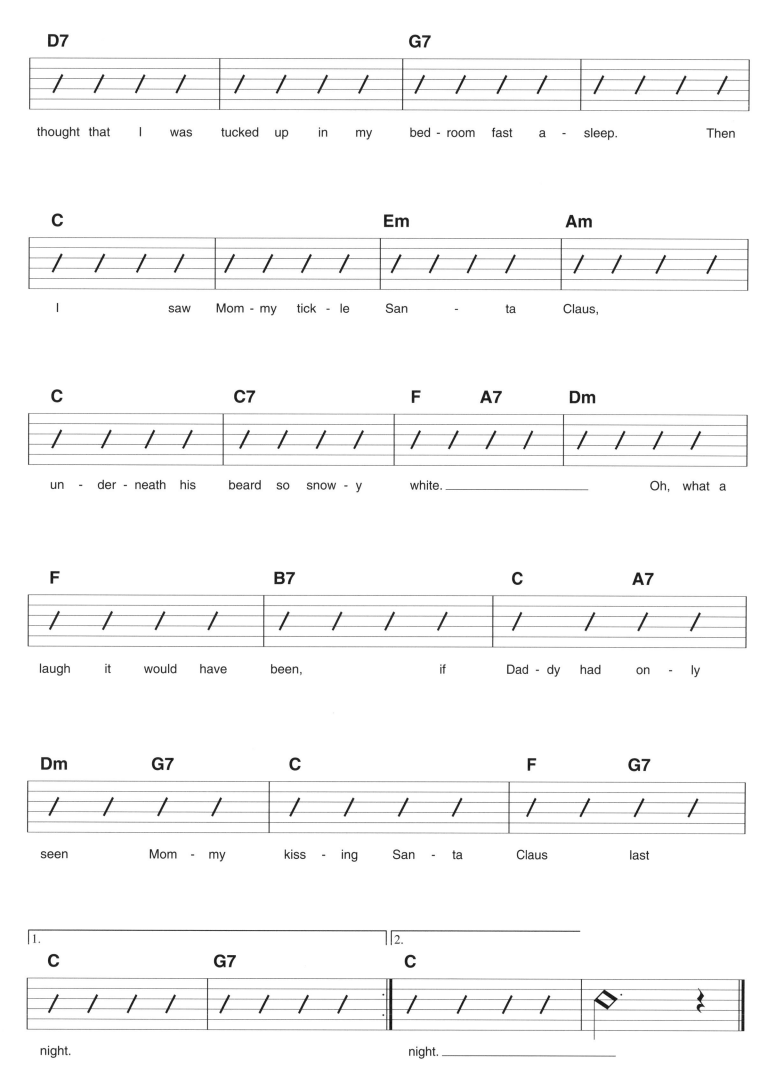

Let It Snow! Let It Snow! Let It Snow!

Words by Sammy Cahn
Music by Jule Styne

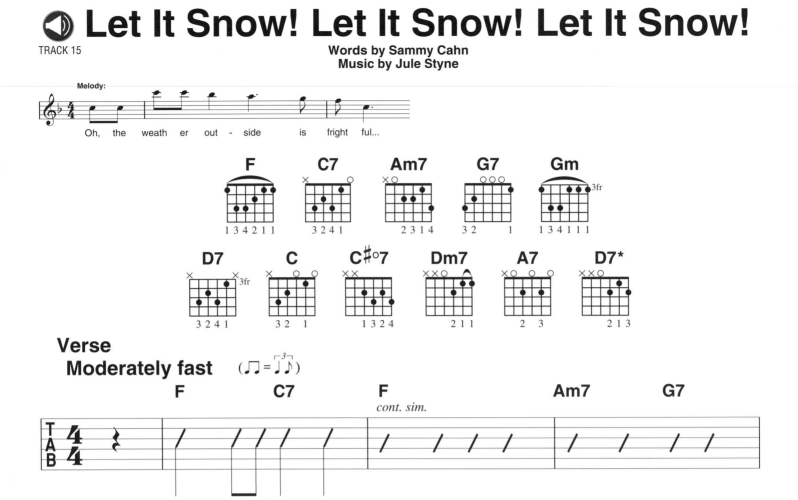

Melody:

Oh, the weath er out - side is fright ful...

F   C7   Am7   G7   Gm

D7   C   C#°7   Dm7   A7   D7*

Verse
Moderately fast

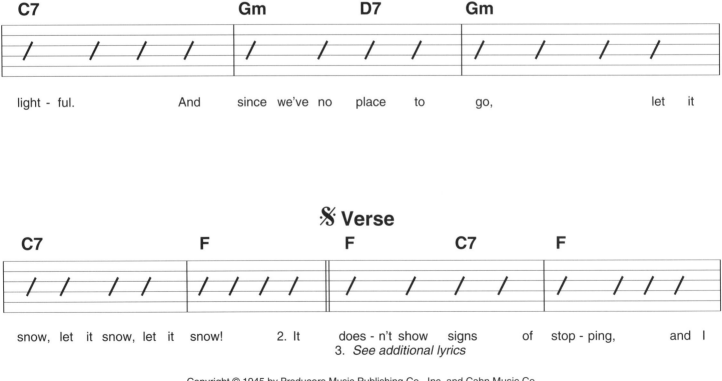

1. Oh, the weath- er out - side is fright - ful, but the fire is so de-

light - ful. And since we've no place to go, let it

snow, let it snow, let it snow! 2. It does - n't show signs of stop - ping, and I
3. *See additional lyrics*

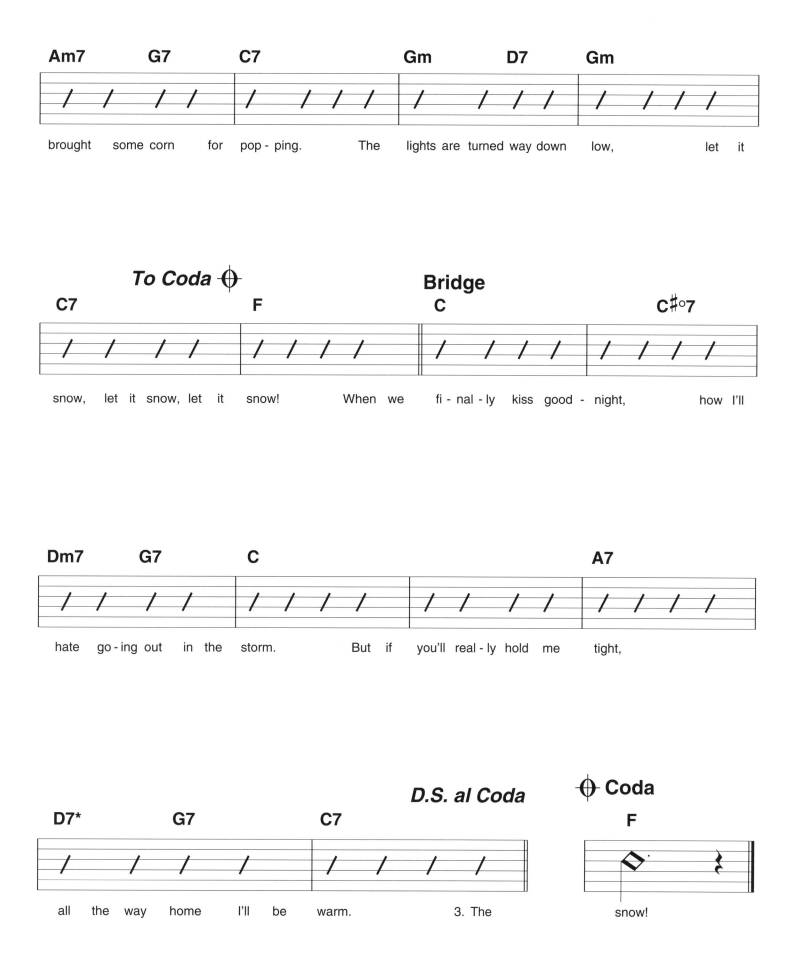

Additional Lyrics

3. The fire is slowly dying
   And, my dear, we're still goodbyeing.
   But as long as you love me so,
   Let it snow, let it snow, let it snow!

Silver Bells

from the Paramount Picture THE LEMON DROP KID
Words and Music by Jay Livingston and Ray Evans

Cit - y side - walks, bus - y side - walks...

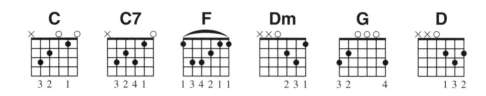

Verse

Moderately

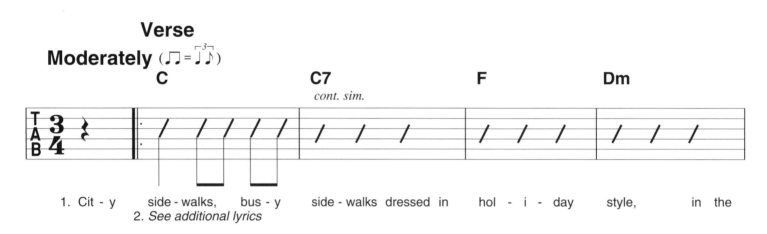

1. Cit - y side - walks, bus - y side - walks dressed in hol - i - day style, in the
2. *See additional lyrics*

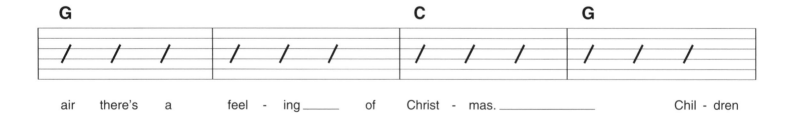

air there's a feel - ing_____ of Christ - mas. _____ Chil - dren

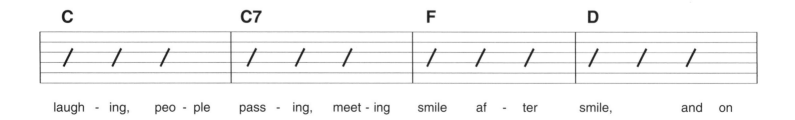

laugh - ing, peo - ple pass - ing, meet - ing smile af - ter smile, and on

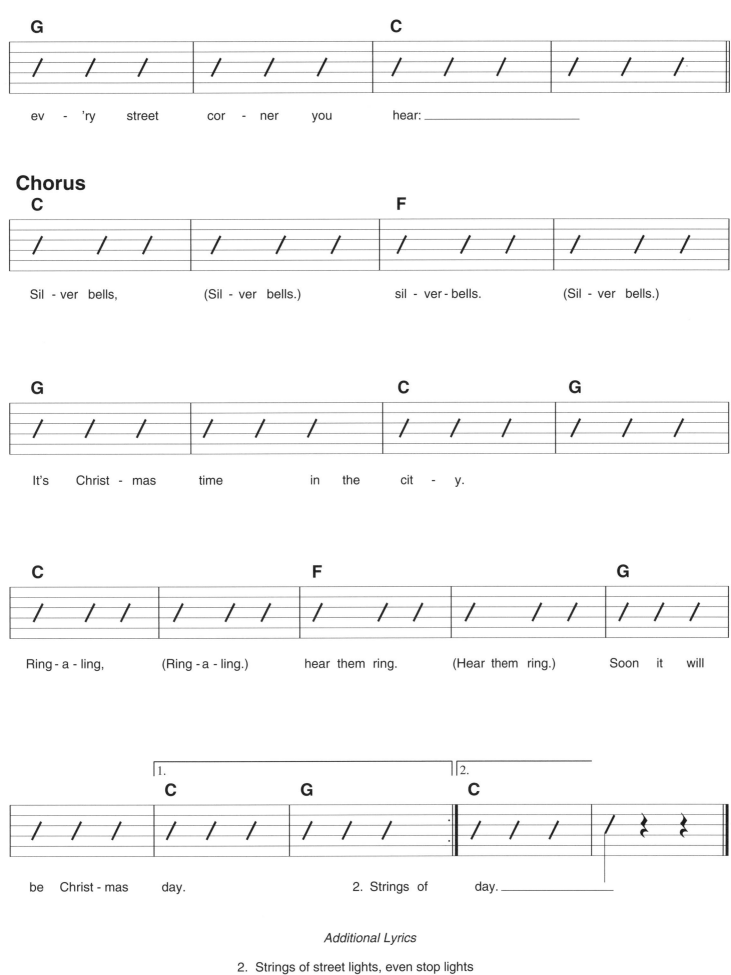

G   **C**

ev - 'ry   street   cor - ner   you   hear: _____

Chorus

C   **F**

Sil - ver bells,   (Sil - ver bells.)   sil - ver - bells.   (Sil - ver bells.)

G   **C**   **G**

It's   Christ - mas   time   in   the   cit - y.

C   **F**   **G**

Ring - a - ling,   (Ring - a - ling.)   hear them ring.   (Hear them ring.)   Soon   it   will

1.   **C**   **G**   2.   **C**

be   Christ - mas   day.   2. Strings of   day. _____

Additional Lyrics

2. Strings of street lights, even stop lights
Blink a bright red and green,
As the shoppers rush home with their treasures.
Hear the snow crunch, see the kids bunch,
This is Santa's big scene,
And above all the bustle you hear:

Rudolph the Red-Nosed Reindeer

TRACK 17

Music and Lyrics by Johnny Marks

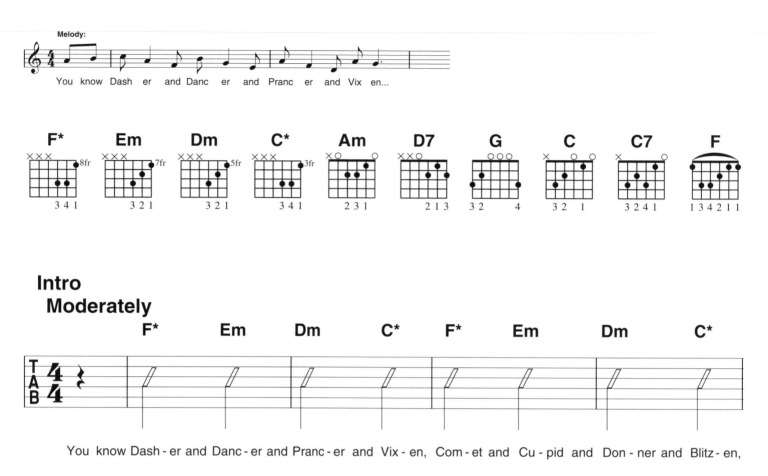

Intro
Moderately

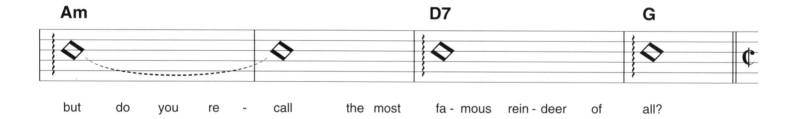

You know Dash-er and Danc-er and Pranc-er and Vix-en, Com-et and Cu-pid and Don-ner and Blitz-en,

but do you re-call the most fa-mous rein-deer of all?

Verse
Lightly

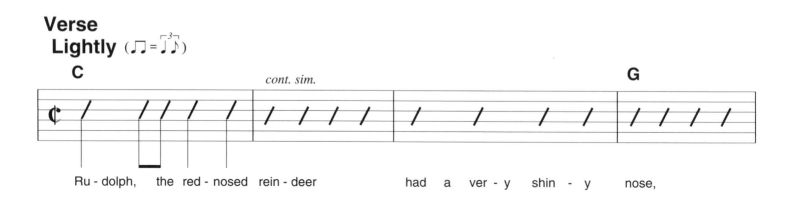

Ru-dolph, the red-nosed rein-deer had a ver-y shin-y nose,

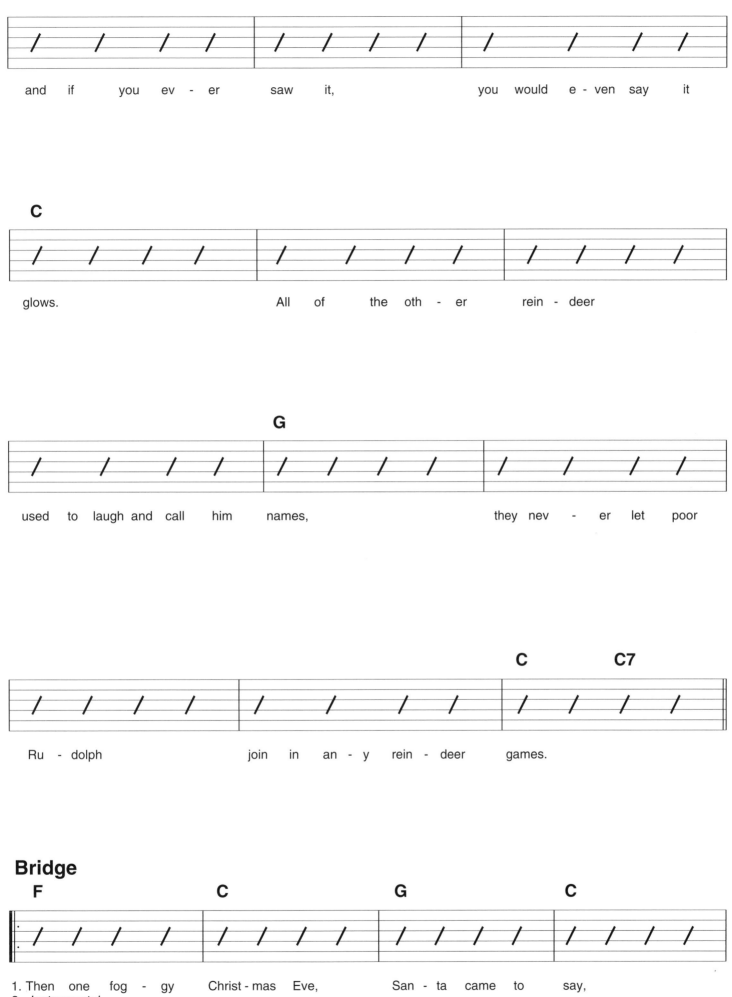

and if   you   ev - er   saw   it,   you   would   e - ven   say   it

C

glows.   All   of   the   oth - er   rein - deer

G

used   to   laugh and   call   him   names,   they   nev - er   let   poor

C   **C7**

Ru - dolph   join   in   an - y   rein - deer   games.

Bridge

F   **C**   **G**   **C**

1. Then   one   fog - gy   Christ - mas   Eve,   San - ta   came   to   say,
2. *Instrumental*

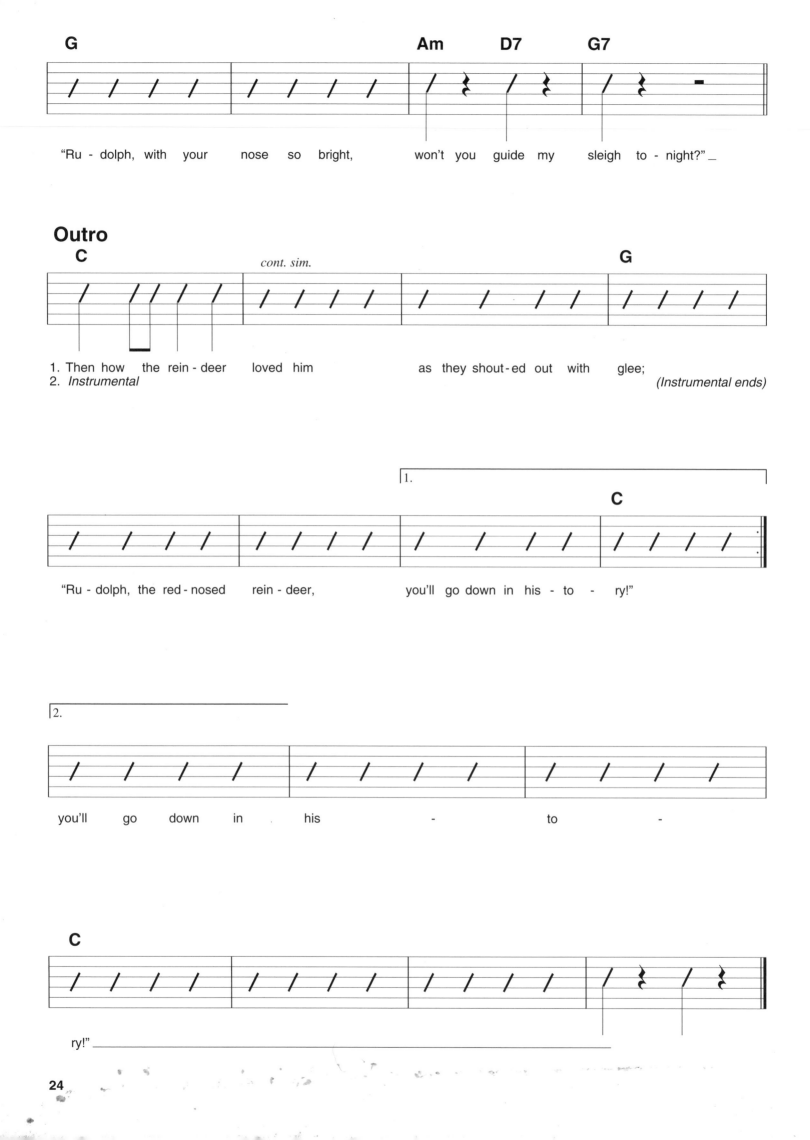

G   **Am**   **D7**   **G7**

"Ru - dolph, with your   nose   so   bright,   won't you   guide   my   sleigh to - night?" __

Outro

C   *cont. sim.*   **G**

1. Then how   the rein - deer   loved him   as they shout - ed out   with   glee;
2. *Instrumental*   *(Instrumental ends)*

1.   **C**

"Ru - dolph, the red - nosed   rein - deer,   you'll go down in his - to - ry!"

2.

you'll   go   down   in   his   -   to   -

C

ry!" _____